Tony Hawk

By Eric Braun

AMAZING ATHLETES

Lerner Publications Company • Minneapolis

This book is available in two editions:
Library binding by Lerner Publications Company
A division of Lerner Publishing Group, Inc.
Soft cover by First Avenue Editions
An imprint of Lerner Publishing Group, Inc.
241 First Avenue North
Minneapolis, MN 55401 U.S.A.

Website address: www.lernerbooks.com

Library of Congress Cataloging-in-Publication Data

Braun, Eric, 1971–
        Tony Hawk / by Eric Braun.
            p.   cm. — (Amazing athletes)
        Summary: Introduces the life and accomplishments of champion skateboarder Tony Hawk.
        Includes bibliographical references and index.
        ISBN-13: 978-0-8225-1367-4 (lib. bdg. : alk. paper)
        ISBN-10: 0-8225-1367-6 (lib. bdg. : alk. paper)
        ISBN-13: 978-0-8225-3686-4 (pbk. : alk. paper)
        ISBN-10: 0-8225-3686-2 (pbk. : alk. paper)
        1. Hawk, Tony—Juvenile literature. 2. Skateboarders—United States—Biography—Juvenile
    literature. [1. Hawk, Tony. 2. Skateboarders.] I. Title. II. Series.
        GV859.813.H39 B73 2004
        796.22'092—dc21   2002013612

Manufactured in the United States of America
5 – BP – 12/1/09

TABLE OF CONTENTS

Excited fans attend the 2003 X Games in Los Angeles, California.

THE GREATEST TRICK

Tony Hawk stood at the top of the U-shaped **ramp,** holding his skateboard. He was about to perform in the 2003 Extreme Games or **X Games** that were being held in Los Angeles, California. Crowds of fans waited for him to start skating. They chanted his name, but Tony didn't look at them.

He was trying again to pull off the greatest **trick** in skateboarding history—the **900.** The 900 is two and a half spins in midair. Tony was the only person who had ever landed the trick at all. But he'd never managed to pull it within a **contest's** time limit. Every time Tony had landed the 900, he had tried and failed so many times, he had gone over the 45 seconds allowed. Could he nail it this time?

Tony fell many times while trying to nail the 900.

Tony successfully performed the 900 within the time limit.

Everybody else had stopped skating. The announcer noted that Tony was skating in the **Vert** (vertical) Best Trick contest. He got up to speed, then fell. He tried again and again. No luck.

Without a break, Tony started all over. He rolled down the wall of the ramp,

Tony had broken several ribs while trying to learn the 900.

across the flat bottom, and up the other wall. He went back and forth a couple of times to get more speed. Then he flew high into the air off the top of the wall. His body spun around two and a half times. He smoothly landed and rolled along the bottom of the ramp. He had landed the 900 on only his fourth try!

The crowd roared. Tony was within the time limit for the first time! He stood on the top of the ramp and heard the applause. Tony Hawk had made skateboarding history.

Tony thanked the fans after his amazing feat.

A young Tony poses in a **skate park**. When he first started skateboarding, he was so skinny that regular knee pads didn't fit him. He wore elbow pads on his knees.

SKATEBOARDING TO THE RESCUE

Tony was born in 1968, the youngest of four children. When Tony was growing up in San Diego, California, people thought he had too much energy. He didn't do well in school. He didn't enjoy team sports like baseball or basketball. If he didn't win a board game, he would throw the board across the room. His mom called him "challenging."

Skateboarding took off in the 1960s, especially in California. By the 1970s, the sport had become hugely popular.

In 1977, when Tony was nine, his brother Steve gave him a skateboard. At first, Tony just goofed around. He couldn't even turn.

But he got better. He began going to a skate park near his house. The skate park had cement **bowls** to ride in. Bowls have steep walls, like ramps. Skating in bowls and ramps is also called vert skating.

Soon, Tony was spending hours at the park every day. He learned tricks and practiced them over and over. "He could never leave a park until he perfected a trick," his brother remembered later.

Tony began to invent tricks of his own. He practiced them a lot until he felt sure he could nail them most of the time.

In full protective gear, Tony posed next to the logo for Tracker Trucks, a major skateboard maker.

GETTING NOTICED

Tony entered his first skateboard contest in 1979, when he was eleven years old. He was so nervous, he thought about skipping it. He had practiced his **run,** or routine of tricks, many times. Still, there would be a lot of people watching.

Tony fell a couple of times during the contest and didn't **place** very well. To place means to finish with a rank, like first or second place, compared to other skaters in the contest. Tony was disappointed. He knew he could skate better. Every day after school, he went to the park to practice. He was already doing daring tricks such as **airs.** Tony even invented some of his own tricks.

To perform an air, a skater rides up the side of a ramp and launches off the top into the air. Then the rider lands back in the ramp again.

In 1980, when Tony was twelve, a skateboard company called Dogtown noticed how well this skinny, blond kid was skating. They decided to **sponsor** him. They gave Tony a Dogtown skateboard and paid for him to enter contests.

Tony shows his stuff in a full pipe (full circle).

Later that year, Dogtown went out of business, and Tony was sponsored by Powell-Peralta. Powell-Peralta was the biggest skateboard company in the country. Its team was called the **Bones Brigade**. Tony was the team's youngest member.

Powell-Peralta designed a Tony Hawk skateboard that carried a bird's skull on it. Whenever somebody bought one, Tony got money.

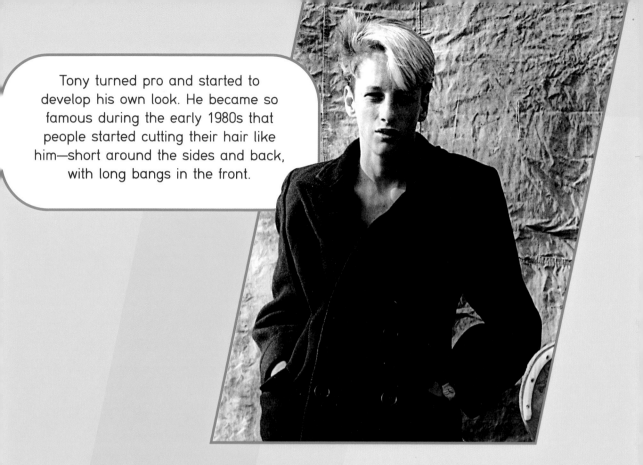

Tony turned pro and started to develop his own look. He became so famous during the early 1980s that people started cutting their hair like him—short around the sides and back, with long bangs in the front.

THE PRO

In 1983, after Tony had turned fourteen, Powell-Peralta thought Tony was ready to become a professional, or **pro.** Tony agreed. As a pro, all his contests would be against other pros. He traveled all over the United States to compete.

By age 16, Tony could pull off almost any trick. But he never stopped practicing to become an even better skater.

In 1985, Tony entered a contest at a park nicknamed The Badlands. It was the most difficult park Tony had ever skated. Tony knew a lot of people thought he wasn't good enough to win at The Badlands. But that day, he skated one of the best runs of his life, and he won. After that, most skaters respected Tony as one of the most talented skaters in the country.

Tony's dad was a big supporter, even when Tony didn't do well in contests. To help Tony get better, Frank Hawk built ramps for him to practice on. He reminded his son that skating should always be fun, no matter how he did in contests.

Tony and his dad were very close. From the beginning, Frank Hawk *(right)* supported Tony's desire to become a great skater.

Not long after the contest at The Badlands, Tony's dad had a heart attack. It was his second one. His dad made it through OK, but Tony worried about him.

Meanwhile, Tony stayed in school. Even though he was a pro skater during his high school years, he was never popular among his classmates. In fact, Tony described himself as an outcast.

In 1986, after Tony graduated from high school, he went on a nationwide **tour** with the Bones Brigade. They drove all over the country and skated in contests. The team made several skate videos, including *The Search for Animal Chin*, that featured Tony.

Tony has admitted that one of the great things about skateboarding not being popular at certain times was "You knew skaters were skating for no reason other than love of the sport."

Thrasher, one of the major skateboarding magazines, did an article about Tony. So did *Sports Illustrated,* a magazine popular with all kinds of sports fans. He was famous even with people who didn't know anything about skating.

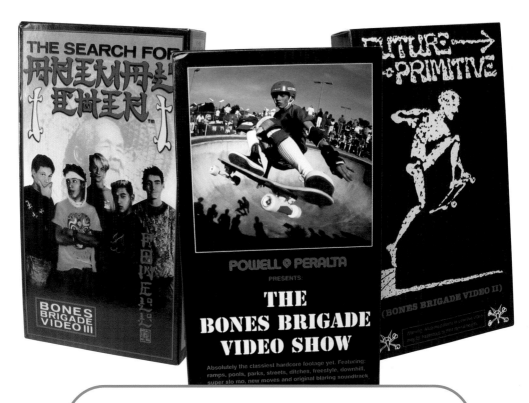

Tony toured with the Bones Brigade in the late 1980s and appeared in a number of skate videos.

Tony holds a signature skateboard and a surfboard.

Skating and Family

By the late 1980s, Tony had many sponsors. Companies paid him a lot of money to help sell their products. He owned two houses and a fancy car. And he won almost every contest he entered.

Tony also fell in love. He married Cindy Dunbar in 1990. In the next few years, skateboarding became much less popular. Suddenly, there were almost no sponsors for Tony. Money became tight. He had to sell his car and one of his houses. Through it all, he kept skating.

The logo of Tony's skateboard company, Birdhouse, appears on his skateboards, helmets, and T-shirts.

In 1991, Tony and one of his friends quit Powell and started a new skateboard company. They called it Birdhouse. Since skating wasn't very popular, Birdhouse didn't do very well. But soon, Tony had other things to think about. His son, Riley, was born in December 1992.

Tony and Cindy loved their son, but things were difficult between them. In 1995, they got divorced.

That same year, ESPN, a TV sports network, started the X Games. Skateboarders, BMX riders, and Rollerbladers all competed in events. Millions of people watched on TV.

Quickly, skateboarding became popular again. Birdhouse became hugely successful. Tony won the X Games vert contest. But once again, something happened to take his mind off skating. His dad died. Tony said he had lost his biggest fan.

Tony takes to the air during the first X Games, held in 1995 in San Diego, California.

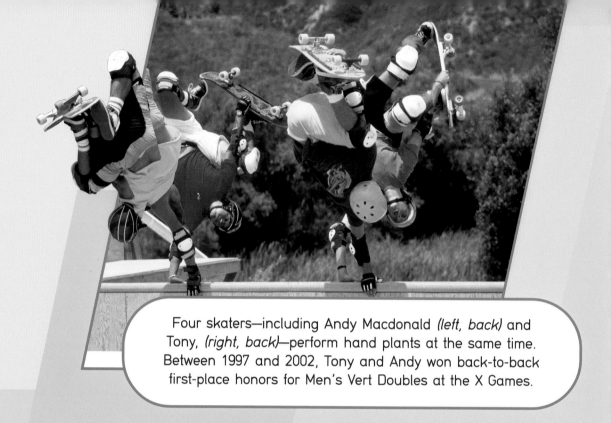

Four skaters—including Andy Macdonald (*left, back*) and Tony, (*right, back*)—perform hand plants at the same time. Between 1997 and 2002, Tony and Andy won back-to-back first-place honors for Men's Vert Doubles at the X Games.

THE WISH LIST

By 1997, skateboarding had become more popular than it had ever been. Tony continued to do very well in contests. He placed first in many competitions. With his partner Andy Macdonald, Tony won the X Games Men's Vert Doubles (two-person performances).

Tony matched career success with changes in his private life. He got married again. He and his new wife, Erin, had a son, Spencer, in 1999. (Keegan, another son, was born in 2001.)

For more than twenty years, Tony had been doing amazing skateboard tricks on ramps. He was the greatest ramp skater of all time. In his mind, he had kept a wish list of tricks he wanted to do. By the late 1990s, he had done almost all of them— except the 900. It was just too hard.

Tony, Erin, and Spencer in 1999

Then, in the 1999 X Games, Tony entered the Vert Best Trick contest. He was going for the 900, no matter what. No one had ever landed it. After many failed tries, Tony had gone beyond the time limit. He didn't care. He again gained speed and flew into the air. He spun two and a half times and almost fell on the landing. But he'd done it!

Tony repeated his feat at the 2002 X Games, but again he went beyond the time limit. At the 2003 X Games—said to be Tony's last—he went for it again. This time, he nailed the 900 within the 45-second limit and won his tenth gold medal.

ESPN invented a new award—the Best Alternative Athlete—which the network gave to Tony in 2000.

Tony has retired officially from competitive skating, but nothing has really changed. He still skates because he loves it. In 2002, Tony organized the first Boom Boom HuckJam tour. It brought together skateboarders, BMX bikers, Motocross riders, and great music. The 2003 Boom Boom HuckJam played across North America to huge crowds. His popular video game, *Tony Hawk's Pro Skater,* is in its fourth edition. And *Tony Hawk's Underground* is his newest video game.

Tony, Andy Mac, and others toured with the Boom Boom HuckJam in the fall of 2003.

Meanwhile, Tony also set up the Tony Hawk Foundation. Part of its mission is to help pay for public skate parks throughout the country.

Tony is a busy skateboarder and family man. He's begun to watch his oldest son, Riley, perform in the sport. And he continues to be grateful for all his success. As Tony has said, "I'm pretty happy with the way things turned out. I mean, I never thought that I could make a career out of skateboarding."

Tony's son Riley has taken up skateboarding too.

Selected Career Highlights

2003 Landed the 900 at X Games within the 45-second time limit
Won Vert Best Trick contest at X Games

2002 With Andy Macdonald, won first place, X Games Men's Vert Doubles
Nailed the 900 at X Games outside of regulation

2001 With Andy Macdonald, won first place, X Games Men's Vert Doubles

2000 With Andy Macdonald, won first place, X Games Men's Vert Doubles

1999 Landed the first 900
Won the Vert Best Trick contest at the X Games
With Andy Macdonald, won first place, X Games Men's Vert Doubles

1998 Won Vert Best Trick at the Hard Rock World Championships
Won third place, X Games vert contest
With Andy Macdonald, won first place X Games Men's Vert Doubles

1997 Won first place, Hard Rock World Championships
Won first place, X Games vert contest
With Andy Macdonald, won first place X Games Men's Vert Doubles

1996 Took second place, X Games vert contest

1995 Won first place, Hard Rock World Championships
Won first place, X Games vert contest

1992 Won first place in the last National Skateboard Association (NSA) Finals

1986 Won first place in Transworld Skateboard Championships

1985 Won first place in The Badlands

1984–1991 Was NSA vert champion eight years in a row

1983 Becomes the NSA vert champion as an amateur
Turned pro at the age of fourteen

1981 Won third place, Variflex Easter Classic

1980 Won fifth place, Del Mar State Finals for boys aged eleven to thirteen

Glossary

air: when a skater launches off the top of a ramp into the air then lands in the ramp again

Bones Brigade: the world-famous skate team sponsored by Powell-Peralta

bowl: a huge, smooth cement hole, like a swimming pool, with steep walls. Skaters ride in it and do tricks at the tops of the walls.

contest: a competition in which skaters take turns doing tricks on a ramp. Judges score the skaters to determine a winner.

900: an extremely tough trick. It requires a skater to launch off the top of a ramp, spin around two and a half times, then land in the ramp again.

place: where a skater ranks in a contest, compared to other skaters in the contest. The winner of a contest takes first place.

pro: an athlete who receives money for participating in an event

ramp: a wooden structure shaped like the letter U. Skaters ride up and down the walls and do tricks. Also known as a half-pipe.

run: the routine of tricks a skater does. In a contest, every skater's run is timed.

skate park: a place with ramps and bowls where skaters can skate

sponsor: a company that pays a skater to help sell its products. A skater might wear a sponsor's clothes, skate on a sponsor's skateboards, or be seen in commercials that advertise the sponsor's products.

tour: a group of skaters who travel to different cities and skate in contests or perform demonstrations

trick: a difficult skateboarding move

vert: short for vertical, refers to skaters skating and doing tricks on a ramp that has straight up-and-down sides

X Games: sponsored by ESPN, an annual series of contests and events for alternative sports

Further Reading & Websites

Powell, Ben. *Skateboarding*. Minneapolis: Lerner Publications Company, 2004.

Stewart, Mark. *One Wild Ride: The Life of Skateboarding Superstar Tony Hawk*. Minneapolis: Twenty-First Century Books, 2002.

Birdhouse Skateboards
http://www.birdhouseskateboards.com
The website of Birdhouse Skateboards. Includes product information and Birdhouse skate team updates

ESPN X Games
http://espn.go.com/action/xgames/index
The X Games website contains a calendar of events, photo gallery, news about athletes and events, and videos.

Sports Illustrated Kids
http://www.sikids.com
The *Sports Illustrated Kids* website that covers all sports, including skateboarding

Thrasher
http://www.thrashermagazine.com
The website of *Thrasher,* a magazine devoted to skateboarding

Tony Hawk Official Website
http://www.tonyhawk.com
Tony's official website has pictures, videos, a biography, a chat room, and links to other skateboarding websites.

Transworld Skateboarding
http://www.skateboarding.com
The website of *Transworld Skateboarding*, a magazine devoted to skateboarding

Index

Photo Acknowledgments

Photographs are used with the permission of: © Tony Donaldson/Icon SMI, pp. 4, 5, 6, 7; © Grant Brittain, pp. 8, 11, 12, 14, 15, 16, 17, 20, 23, 24, 28, 29; © Don Morley/EMPICS Sports Photo Agency, p. 10; © Todd Strand/ Independent Picture Service, pp. 19, 27; © David Leeds/Getty Images, p. 22; © Duomo/CORBIS, p. 25.

Cover: © David Leeds/Getty Images.